ideals®
CHRISTMAS

Hang a bow upon the door,
A star upon the tree;
Light a candle where its glow
Can guide a friend to thee.
Share a cup and memories sweet
And dreams that make you glad.
Celebrate the merriest
Christmas that you've had.

—*Betty Wallace Scott*

IDEALS PUBLICATIONS
NASHVILLE, TENNESSEE

Christmastime Is Here

Margaret Rorke

All is hustle-bustle,
Feel it in the air?
Hear the tissue rustle,
Crushed to cloak with care
Something as a token
For a person dear,
Wrapping love unspoken.
Christmastime is here.

See the tinsel glisten,
Hear the sound of bells;
Pause a bit and listen,
Nothing else excels.
Joy is in suspension.
Hark the carols clear
Taking turns to mention
Christmastime is here.

Note the light aglowing
In a youngster's eyes.
There's no way of knowing
How to price that prize.
Candles fade beside it.
It illumes the sphere.
There's no way to hide it . . .
Christmastime is here.

Fellow folk are kinder,
We are kinder too;
Each a would-be finder
Of some good to do.
This, the grand sensation,
Rises once a year
With the realization
Christmastime is here.

A Christmas Card
Daisy Wakefield

I saw enthralled this morn at dawn,
A lovely Christmas card.
It made the world a magic place
Where angels stand on guard.

'Twas etched in simple blue and white,
By One Who knew His trade,
Below He cast a mantle white,
Above the sky He made.

The trees He dressed as lords of old,
In ermine robes so fair,
And o'er it all the sun did shine,
Dispersing woe and care.

It was a lovely Christmas card,
Which I would send to you,
If I could only say with words
What He in beauty drew.

Christmas Cards
Ruth M. Bryan

Christmas cards with pine and holly,
Santa Claus all fat and jolly,
A star above a manger bed,
Wise men following where it led.

Christmas cards relate the story
Of Jesus' birth and angels' glory,
Of peace on earth, the hope of men,
Of light that guides the world again.

Christmas cards from near and far
Seek my door as by a star,
But they are more than cards to me—
They're friends around
my Christmas tree.

THE CHRISTMAS CARDS AND LETTERS,
THE GIFTS FROM NEAR AND FAR
ARE SYMBOLS OF ANOTHER GIFT
REVEALED BENEATH A STAR.
—Alice Kennelly Roberts

Photograph by
Nancy Matthews

ON THE ROOF.

THE TEA SET

Patricia Penton Leimbach

Twenty-one piece set of blue lusterware . . . $2.98" was what it said alongside the picture in the Sears, Roebuck Christmas catalogue. We were overwhelmed at such value and set our sights on scaring up the three bucks and some odd cents that must be figured in for tax and postage. It was the biggest gift we'd ever tackled for Mama; up to that point we'd been satisfied with the cross-stitch on burlap or the file-card holders or the black construction-paper silhouettes that Miss Zilch or Miss Drechsler or Mrs. Smith dreamed up to motivate us between Thanksgiving and Christmas.

Bill and I had a little money left from selling bittersweet and John made up the rest from his paper route earnings.

With our sister Mary's help we filled out the form and sent it off with a money order procured from the mailman by putting a Please Blow Horn sign in the mailbox. This had to be accomplished on Saturday, when Mama was gone to market. Then the vigil began. Let's see—two days for the order to get to Chicago, a couple of days to process it, three or four days coming back, and a Sunday in between. At the most it ought to come in nine days.

Every day we got out the catalogue and turned it to the dog-eared page where our treasure was pictured. "What do you think of that, Mama?" asked Bill, with thinly disguised braggadocio. "Wouldn't you just love to have something like that around here?" Our tea set was as well kept a secret as a case of mumps.

As good luck would have it, the package arrived two weeks to the day from when we ordered. Saturday again, and Mama was at market, so we set the box on a chair and dived in with all six fists. Not a very big box for twenty-one pieces! But all the same, big enough to make quite some impression under the tree.

We extracted the pieces, one by one, scattering excelsior all over Mary's clean dining room. She was as excited as we and scarcely scolded us for what at other times would have unleashed a tirade.

First the cream pitcher, then the sugar bowl. "The lid? . . . Oh, here." Then the wondrous teapot—shimmering blue laced with a spray of pinkish-red blossoms. To our chagrin one of the cups was a tissue-paper wad of broken pieces. Oh well, even a twenty-piece tea set was not to be sneezed at. Maybe some adjustment could be made.

We counted them all, wrapping them again in the tissue and laboriously fitting them back in the excelsior, hastening to banish all traces before Mom got home. We wrapped the box in two or three pieces of last year's Christmas paper, closing the stubborn flaps with Christmas seals that came "free" in the mail. We adorned it royally with old ribbon untangled from the wad and then hid it away in Mary's closet.

Everything else about that Christmas pales before the splendid moment when Mama opened the box from Sears, Roebuck.

Photograph by Jessie Walker

I don't really remember how she reacted. I'm sure it was a convincing show. It didn't occur to us (as I'm sure it did to her) to wonder where in our crowded cupboard she was going to put twenty pieces of china "Made in Japan."

We used the tea set from time to time and the pieces disappeared. The cream pitcher went early in the game, then the six plates, the five cups, the saucers. The remnants moved gradually upward in the cupboard.

When we went through Mama's fifty-seven year accumulation of "things," way up in the rear of the top shelf of the kitchen cupboard we unearthed the lid to a sugar bowl long gone and the blue luster teapot. Its spout was held on precariously with Scotch tape; no tea has poured from it for years. But too precious, obviously, to discard were the fragments of a Christmas memory more cherished than the gift had ever been.

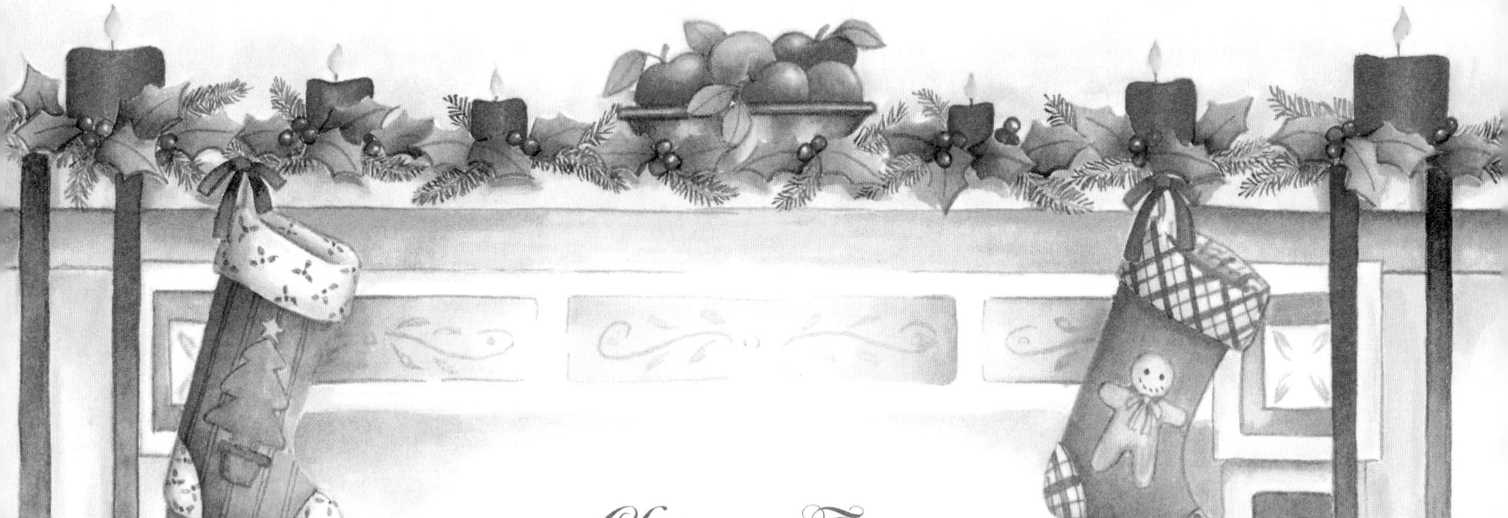

Christmas Time

Dorothy Minner

The holly and the mistletoe
Are once again in season.
People raise their voice in song
For no apparent reason.

On all the busy city streets
We see the cheerful throngs;
While carolers in scarfs
and gloves
Repeat the well-worn songs.

The little boys and girls
have been
As good as they could be.
Anticipation in their eyes
Is wonderful to see.

In the kitchen Mother sings
Of far-off Bethlehem,
While Dad is checking
colored lights—
There is a tree to trim.

Oh, Christmas is a happy time—
It fills our hearts with cheer
And brings a glow that lingers on
Throughout the bright
New Year.

December

Harriet F. Blodgett

Oh! Holly branch and mistletoe
And Christmas chimes where'er we go
And stockings pinned up in a row—
These are thy gifts, December!

And if the year has made thee old
And silvered all thy locks of gold,
Thy heart has never been a-cold
Or known a fading ember.

The whole world is a Christmas tree,
And stars its many candles be.
Oh! Sing a carol joyfully
The year's great feast in keeping!

For once, on a December night
An angel held a candle bright
And led three wise men by its light
To where a Child was sleeping.

Photograph by Miki Duisterhof/Botanica/Jupiter Images

The Buying of Gifts
Grace Noll Crowell

When I was a child on my father's farm,
And Christmastime drew near,
I would trudge through the snow
    to the little town . . .
Oh, the memory is quite clear
Of the little girl with a quarter to spend
For parents, for brother, and sister,
    and friend.

My scarlet mittens and scarlet hood
Were white with glistening snow,
My eyes were shining with eagerness,
My frost-bright cheeks aglow,
As I went gladly, hurrying down
To the novelty store in the little town.

And oh, the rapture, the sheer delight!
The shop's small windows shone
With beautiful things . . .
    and there was I
With a quarter all my own!
I searched—and will wonders
    never cease?
I found five gifts for a nickel apiece.

Such beautiful gifts! And trudging home
Through the winter dusk, I knew
A joy and a glowing happiness
That has lasted the long years through.
For something of that far Christmastime
Stayed in my heart, and it still is mine.

CHRISTMAS TOY SHOP *by Sheila Sanford. Image from DDFA.com*

SAND TARTS

Kendall Crolius

My brother and sister and I grew up having wonderful things going on in my mother's kitchen. What I remember us all making together is Christmas cookies. There is the Christmas cookie recipe that is the same one my mother's grandparents made. I come from long lines of Germans on many sides of the family so: sand tarts. I make them now, and I try to do it with my kids and my sister's daughter and my goddaughter, because there are jobs for everyone. The mom has to roll the dough out, the older children cut the cookies and get them onto the cookie sheets. The cookies also have to be brushed with beaten egg white and sprinkled with cinnamon sugar, and then there's the coveted job of placing the piece of pecan on top. It's a whole hierarchy; you have to prove yourself to graduate to the next job. When you're really little, it doesn't occur to you that sprinkling the cinnamon sugar isn't the most fun thing. You're so happy doing that and licking the cinnamon sugar off your fingers, but there's a point where you go, "Hey, wait a minute. What's that paintbrush thing called? I want to do that."

Several days before this past Christmas, I was making cookies with my sister and my daughter and my niece and talking about the whole system of it. My sister was kind of smiling quietly and looking at me, and I was talking and talking. Finally, my sister said, "That's great, but do you realize I'm forty-three years old and you've never let me roll out the dough?" We got absolutely hysterical about it, because it was true. I'm the older sister, and it's always been my job, since I took it over from my mother. So my sister, this year, did get to roll out the dough. The cookies turned out just fine, I must say. But she rolled them out and said, "Whew, well that was fun; now I'm going to go back to supervising the pecans and the sugar." And I think I may have permanently regained control of the dough rolling.

My sister and I actually toyed with the idea of not making Christmas cookies this year: "If you can't do it Saturday, and I can't do it Sunday, next week is the Christmas pageant, maybe we don't have time, but we have to make time to do it!" It would not be Christmas without sand tarts; the whole package would just fall apart without them. There's something very reassuring about the annual repetition of it. Your sense of smell is connected to the primal, reptilian part of your brain. Smells are supposed to evoke a memory more directly and more dramatically than any other sense. The smell of Christmas cookies baking—not just eating them, but what the house smells like when you're preparing them—is half the fun. And eating the first Christmas cookie, warm off the baking sheet, and taking a cookie or two out of the tin in the kitchen all during the Christmas season. We still leave cookies for Santa on Christmas Eve, and he still eats them. One year, in a late evening daze of tidying up, I washed the plate we'd left the cookies on. My husband, Stephen, caught my mistake before we finally went to bed, and we left another crumby plate on the mantle.

Photograph by Jessie Walker

Family Recipes

Chocolate-Topped Peanut Butter Cookies

1	14-ounce can sweetened condensed milk	2	cups Bisquick baking mix
¾	cup peanut butter		Granulated sugar
1	teaspoon vanilla extract	36	chocolate kisses

In a medium bowl, combine sweetened condensed milk, peanut butter, and vanilla. Stir in Bisquick, and refrigerate 15 minutes.

Preheat oven to 375°F. Roll batter into 1-inch balls; roll in granulated sugar and place on ungreased baking sheet. Bake 6 to 8 minutes. Immediately place chocolate kiss in the center of each cookie. Cool on baking sheet 2 minutes; transfer to cooling rack and cool completely. Makes 3 dozen cookies.

Fruit-and-Nut Bars

⅓	cup all-purpose flour	1½	cups dates, pitted and quartered
⅛	teaspoon baking soda	1	cup dried apricots, chopped
⅛	teaspoon baking powder	½	cup dried cherries or cranberries
¼	teaspoon salt	1	egg
⅓	cup light brown sugar	½	teaspoon vanilla extract
1½	cups walnuts, chopped		

Preheat oven to 325°F. In a large bowl, combine flour, baking soda, baking powder, and salt. Stir in the brown sugar, walnuts, and dried fruit, coating fruit and nuts well.

In a small bowl, combine the egg and vanilla and beat until light colored and thick. Add to the fruit and nut mixture, and stir until all the fruit and nut pieces are coated with the batter. Spread evenly into a foil-lined 8 x 8-inch baking pan.

Bake 35 to 40 minutes or until golden brown and pulling away from the sides of the pan. Cool in pan on a wire rack. When cooled, lift the bars from the pan by the edges of the aluminum foil. Slice into 2-inch squares. Makes 16 bars.

SAND TARTS

2 cups butter, softened
2¾ cups granulated sugar, divided
2 large eggs, beaten
4 cups all-purpose flour
4 teaspoons ground cinnamon
1 egg white, lightly beaten
Pecan halves

In a large bowl, cream butter and 2½ cups sugar. Add the eggs and mix thoroughly. Slowly add flour, working it in well. Cover and chill overnight.

Preheat oven to 350°F. In a small bowl, mix together remaining sugar and cinnamon; set aside. On a lightly floured board, roll out dough to ¼-inch thickness. Cut out cookies with holiday cookie cutters, or cut out diamond-shaped cookies using a sharp knife. Brush cookies with egg white and sprinkle with cinnamon sugar; press a pecan half into center of each cookie. Bake about 10 minutes. Makes 3 to 4 dozen cookies.

GINGERBREAD SNOWFLAKES

6 cups all-purpose flour
1 teaspoon baking soda
½ teaspoon baking powder
1 cup unsalted butter
1 cup dark brown sugar
4 teaspoons ground ginger
4 teaspoons ground cinnamon
1½ teaspoons ground cloves
1 teaspoon ground black pepper
1½ teaspoons coarse salt
2 large eggs
1 cup unsulfured molasses
Icing, colored sugar, or
sprinkles, optional

In a large bowl, sift together flour, baking soda, and baking powder; set aside. In a large bowl, cream butter and sugar until fluffy. Mix in spices and salt, then eggs and molasses. Add flour mixture; mix until just combined. Divide dough into thirds; wrap each in plastic wrap. Refrigerate until cold, about 1 hour.

Preheat oven to 350°F. Roll out dough on a lightly floured work surface to ¼-inch thickness. Cut with a 4 to 5-inch snowflake-shape cookie cutter. Space 2 inches apart on baking sheets lined with parchment paper, and refrigerate until firm, about 15 minutes. Bake cookies until crisp but not dark, 12 to 14 minutes. Let cool on sheets on wire racks.

Once cookies are cool, decorate with icing, colored sugar, or sprinkles if desired. Makes about 3 dozen cookies.

Christmas Is Here

Deborah A. Bennett

The wind is chill
against the pane,
the earth is icy
down the lane,
the sky is full and
gray and near,
but little we care
for Christmas is here!

December's long with
darkened days,
and springtime sleeps
where the garden lays;
the vale's gone silent,
stark, and mere,
but little we care
for Christmas is here!

The drifts of snow
have hid the porch,
have hid the woodland's
autumn torch.
The bluebird's song
we long to hear,
but little we care
for Christmas is here!

NOW CHRISTMAS IS COME,
    LET'S BEAT UP THE DRUM,
AND CALL ALL OUR NEIGHBORS
    TOGETHER,
AND WHEN THEY APPEAR,
LET US MAKE THEM
    SUCH CHEER
AS WILL KEEP OUT THE
    WIND AND THE WEATHER.
                    –Washington Irving

Detail from HOLIDAY CARDINAL *by Sam Timm.*
Artwork courtesy of the artist and Wild Wings

CHRISTMAS IS MANY THINGS

Lucille Crumley

Christmas is many things to many people. To me, Christmas means glowing and beautiful things. It means getting the house ready for love. It is the pine tree selected with care. It is trimming the tree with balls and bells, with silver horns and tinsel, with twinkle lights and a smiling angel on top; all of these, gathered through the years, to recall some special Christmas past.

It means hurrying among crowds of people, from store to store, in search of the right gift for someone you love. It means wrapping, with yards of lovely paper and ribbon, that special gift for a special someone.

It means unwrapping the Christmas feeling that we hold in our hearts; the feeling we promised to use more freely during the past year; but somehow got boxed up with the holiday decorations and stored away.

It is pressing your face close to a shop window filled with toys and remembering that red sled you so wanted a long time ago. All the years, between then and now, rush in with sweet nostalgia.

Christmas is the little girl caressing her new doll. It is a little boy in ecstasy over a new bike. It is your son, coming home after two years in a foreign war, and finding everything the same with those at home. It is a granddaughter writing "Merry Christmas" in a little girl's wobbly scrawl on your frosted windowpane.

Christmas is a table decorated with poinsettias and loaded with good things to eat. It is grandmas and grandpas, aunts and uncles and children and grandchildren, gathered around the table; and one special little boy asking the blessing.

Christmas is the joy from Bethlehem when we sing "Silent Night" and "Joy to the World." It is the warmth and faith we feel when our children sing carols at school or take part in the age-old tableau of the nativity that lifts us out of the present time and carries us far away to Bethlehem.

Christmas is going outside on a crisp Christmas night and looking upward to the cold, shining stars and remembering the one great star that led to the birthplace of a Child who was the Bread of Life and the Light of the World.

Photograph by William H. Johnson

Christmas Charm
June Masters Bacher

The attic's locked with secrets;
The air is charmed with spice;
And every ugly word or deed
Somehow comes out nice.

The whispers in the parlor
Echo to girl and boy
That hearts are warmed with loving—
And stockings stuffed with joy.

Gift-Wrapped with Love
Helen Darby Berning

It takes more than tinsel,
A wreath, or a bell
To weave all the magic
That Christmas can spell.

Old friends who remember
With cards through the years;
The Bethlehem message
To dry the world's tears;

The pattern of snowflakes
And frost's silvered lace;
A family together
With heads bowed in grace;

A child's wide-eyed wonder
At stars on a tree—
All these make the carols
Sing Christmas for me.

Photograph by Jessie Walker

A Small-Town Christmas

Haven Kimmel

There was never a town more beautiful at Christmas than Mooreland, Indiana. We didn't hang decorations on every telephone pole, the way some towns do, and we didn't have a community Christmas tree. Instead, Shorty Gard, whose wife, Kathleen, played the piano at our church, used to cover their entire house with colored bulbs. It was a small house—in fact, I think it had formerly been a garage—but still. Sitting in the middle of a field the way it did, and shining out of the darkness, it was a little revelation. Three times a week during the holiday season my dad would say, "Let's go drive past Shorty's house," and we'd put on layers and layers of clothes and pile in the truck and drive a block down Jefferson Street, where the town ended and the country began.

Every year our church went caroling, and I would walk down the cold, dark streets next to my mom. The elm trees that lined Broad Street, meeting in the middle to form a canopy of leaves in the summer, were now just bare branches through which I could see the winter sky, sometimes bright with stars like ice, and sometimes dense and heavy with coming snow. It seemed there was someone home at every house, and as we stood in the street or on the porch, the men gathered in the back with their deep and smooth voices, the altos assembled behind my thin soprano, I would be washed in the heat that escaped through the front doors of all my fellow townspeople. Inside I would see the delicate decorations most people chose: candles, a wreath on the mantle, poinsettias on the windowsills. No one else went as far as Shorty; it was his role to please us so much. There was something perfect about the barest flicker of a candle in an upstairs window, there was something so lovely and restrained about the smallest changes. There was a suggestion in every house, just behind every door, that something miraculous was about to happen.

Photograph by William H. Johnson

Christmas Snowman
Elisabeth Weaver Winstead

The Christmas snowman sends a glow
Across the sparkling, silver snow.

A green wool hat is on his head,
His buttoned vest is cherry red.

His carrot nose is long and thin;
Deep dimples dance about his chin.

He's wider around than he is tall;
He seems to have no neck at all.

His smoke-black eyes are lumps of coal;
His mouth made from a crimson bowl.

His corncob teeth are large and round
To hold a pipe turned upside down.

Long broomstick arms touch frozen ground
Where wind sweeps shattered straws around.

Feathered snowflakes flutter by
The snowman etched against the sky.

Our Christmas snowman quickly starts
Bright Christmas magic in our hearts.

Angels in the Snow
Irma Sanborn

We used to play in winter's snow
By making angel wings you know.
We'd lie so still with arms up high,
In snow that was so smooth
    and dry.

Then through the snow, all white
    and deep,

Our arms so carefully we'd sweep
Until our hands o'erhead we'd bring;
Each arm had made an angel's wing.

Then up we'd rise with greatest care,
Not to disturb the images there,
And gazed with wonder at the row
Of Christmas angels in the snow.

SNOW ANGELS *by Robert Duncan. Image © Robert Duncan Studios*

In Search of a Christmas Tree

Susan G. Sharp-Anderson

We climbed out of the car, all bundled in our down jackets. My husband, Ray, stopped long enough to sling the saw over his shoulder before we moved into the forest. Twigs and downed branches impeded our way, but our two boys, Eric and Marcotte, aged eleven and six, sped through the underbrush like deer. I stepped slowly on the path, holding the small hand of our three-year-old daughter, Elisabeth. Thus the 1981 adventure of our annual search for a Christmas tree was initiated.

Each year, with a $2.00 permit from the National Forest Office, we trekked through the woods, the ingredients for hot chocolate and churros set out and waiting for our return in the kitchen at home. These were the requirements for cutting in the forest and decorating at the house. The children would sometimes complain about having to go out into the cold, but they were always proud of the one tree they chose, perfect in their eyes.

The particular day when we first began the tradition was cloudy, not unusual in Oregon, but there was crispness in the air, which smelled of snow. The uncertainty about snowfall made the quest more exciting.

The tradition continued each year, and each year, we thought it would be easy to pick a tree, but it never was. We'd find a beautiful little fir and then decide it wasn't big enough. We'd see another and then decide that it was too big. Many times Ray agreed with one child that he had found the perfect tree, and then the other would squeal, "No, over here! Here's a better one!"

There were always so many trees that it was hard to decide upon one. And growing in the wild, they often had strange shapes. We'd think that the tree looked great, but then the backside would be flat with no significant branches.

Eventually, we would all agree on one, sometimes because we were so cold that we just wanted to go home and sometimes because it truly was the nicest tree we'd seen. Ray would saw off the trunk at ground level, occasionally assisted by Eric or Marcotte. With cheers, we watched it fall. Then the boys scrambled to drag it to the car. Ray would grab the base, while the boys took posts at the middle and the "star end."

Tying the tree to the roof of the car has always been a challenge, and that was definitely the case on this, the first time we ever attempted it. But, with blankets, ropes, and the orange permit tied to a branch, we finally made our way back through the forest to the main road, which would lead us home. It was a cold but fun romp through the woods, and we were happy to warm our fingers on the car heater with the promise of hot chocolate and pastry when we arrived home again.

At the house, we put the tree into the tree stand and immediately watered it. None of us wanted our hard work to dry out. While I started preparing the refreshments, Ray helped Eric string the lights. This job took organization and skill to make sure that they included every branch.

Painting by David Lenz. Image from Ideals Publications

Elisabeth picked out ornaments and handed them to Marcotte, although she occasionally wanted to hang the ornaments herself. The cat watched sleepily from the corner of the hearth, knowing that when everyone was in bed, he could play with the lower items without reprimand.

We always invited our neighbors, the Beals, to come over to share our hot food and drink, as well as to see the handiwork of nature and children. Bree and Erin, who were Marcotte's and Elisabeth's age, played happily with our children, while the adults shared their latest stories in front of the fire and newly decorated tree.

As we sat around the first tree in 1981, we were in high spirits. When the hot chocolate was ready and the churros—fluted tubes of pastry sprinkled with powdered sugar—were draining on paper towels, I set up a tray and took our treats into the living room. Everyone paused what they were doing to enjoy the companionship and sweetness of the snack.

Every year since that first snowy trek in 1981, we have annually made the sojourn. The family continues to grow, but the tradition remains the same.

Little Tree
e. e. cummings

little tree
little silent Christmas tree
you are so little
you are more like a flower

who found you in the green forest
and were you very sorry to come away?
see   i will comfort you
because you smell so sweetly

i will kiss your cool bark
and hug you safe and tight
just as your mother would,
only don't be afraid

look   the spangles
that sleep all the year in a dark box
dreaming of being taken out and allowed to shine,
the balls the chains red and gold the fluffy threads,

put up your little arms
and i'll give them all to you to hold
every finger shall have its ring
and there won't be a single place dark or unhappy

then when you're quite dressed
you'll stand in the window for everyone to see
and how they'll stare!
oh but you'll be very proud

and my little sister and i will take hands
and looking up at our beautiful tree
we'll dance and sing
"Noel Noel"

Christmas Tree
Laurence Smith

Star over all
Eye of the night
Stand on my tree
Magical sight
Green under frost
Green under snow
Green under tinsel

Glitter and glow
Appled with baubles
Silver and gold
Spangled with fire
Warm over cold.

The Christmas Pine Tree
Boris Pasternak

I love her to tears, at sight, from the first,
As she comes from the woods—
      in storm and snow.
So awkward her branches, the shiest of firs!
We fashion her threads unhurriedly, slow.
Her garments of silvery gossamer lace,
Patterns of tinsel, and spangles aglow
From branch unto branch down to the base.

THROUGH MY WINDOW

CHRISTMAS TREE TALES

Pamela Kennedy

From the time I was a little girl, my favorite holiday memories always involved our Christmas tree. Thick with needles and the pungent, crisp scent of evergreen, it was the tree that transformed the everyday air in our house into something magical. After the tree was decorated, my greatest delight was to lie under it, gazing up through the shimmering lights and dark green branches, breathing deeply of the intoxicating fragrance, lost in holiday fantasies.

When I was nine years old, my father lost his job in Seattle and that October we moved to Southern California. I was devastated and homesick. I missed my friends and relatives. I didn't like palm trees or cacti. . . . The only thing I looked forward to during that long and lonely fall was Christmas. Things would be wonderful at Christmas. We'd have a huge evergreen tree, just like always, and I'd lie under it and pretend I was back in Washington. Unaware of the financial realities my parents faced, it never occurred to me that they couldn't afford a Christmas tree.

December came and I asked when we'd get our tree. Mother gave me vague answers about waiting until closer to Christmas. Then one day I came home from school and there it was—a scrawny evergreen branch stuck in a pot filled with gravel.

"But that's not a Christmas tree!" I looked at the pitiful thing and my eyes filled with tears.

My mother, a loving, but no-nonsense kind of woman, sat me down on the couch and put her arm around me. "Daddy is working very hard but we just don't have enough money to spend on a Christmas tree this year. You need to be a big girl now and try to understand. Can you do that?"

I looked at the little evergreen branch and nodded, suddenly feeling a bit afraid. I had been allowed a glimpse of the adult world and discovered a scary place where beloved traditions were taken hostage by harsh reality.

Resolving to hide my disappointment, I did a fairly good job . . . until Christmas Eve. As my father tucked me into bed and listened to my prayers, I began to cry. "I'm sorry," I sniffed. "It's just that I really miss the Christmas tree."

He dried my tears with the edge of the sheet. "I know, pumpkin, I know."

I hugged him, feeling safe again in his strong familiar arms and suddenly guilty for my selfishness. He rearranged the covers under my chin and smiled. "Sleep tight," he said as he left my room.

When I woke up, the early morning sun was peeking under the window shades. "Christmas!" I jumped out of bed and ran to the living room, then gasped! There was a huge evergreen, lights blazing, covered with tinsel and ornaments! I squealed and spun around, then ran into my parents' arms. "Where did it come from?"

Mother shrugged and grinned at Daddy, "Must be Christmas magic!" he announced.

I didn't care how it got there. Suddenly I had the feeling that all would be well. It wasn't until years later that I learned how my father had gone out that Christmas Eve and scouted around to find a Christmas tree lot still open. He had told the proprietor about his daughter's disappointment and the fellow, overcome with Christmas generosity, and no doubt concerned about having to dispose of his wilting inventory, let my dad haul off his biggest tree for one dollar. My parents had stayed up most of the night decorating the behemoth.

Now, fifty years later, I thought about that tree as we anticipated our daughter's arrival home from college for Christmas. When she was an infant, we moved into an old, two-story wood frame house with bedrooms upstairs and a belching furnace in the basement. For safety reasons, that Christmas we opted for an artificial Douglas fir that we dubbed "Bartholomew." Throughout her life, we had moved several times, but one thing never changed. We had decorated that same artificial tree every one of the past twenty years and for

her, that old tree *was* Christmas. Unfortunately, we ascertained around Thanksgiving that despite being well loved, "Bartholomew" clearly wouldn't make it through another Yuletide. So, in early December, we purchased a gorgeous new tree, complete with hundreds of sparkling lights. We decorated it with all of our favorite keepsake ornaments and set aside our treetop angel for our daughter to put in place as always.

"Bartholomew II" was beautiful, but we still had some misgivings about our daughter's reaction.

I was setting up the crèche a few days before her arrival when my husband wandered in from the garage bearing an eighteen-inch artificial evergreen, attached to a square wooden stand.

"What's that?" I asked as he placed it next to the stable.

"Annie's tree." He replied. "I couldn't dump old 'Bart' completely, so I saved the top section. Besides, when she has a home of her own someday, she can take a part of her past with her."

I smiled, looking at the little tree, remembering how my Daddy had also recognized my need for Christmas traditions so many decades ago.

"She's lucky," I sighed, leaning into the familiar embrace of my husband's arm. "And so am I. Merry Christmas, love."

Christmas Once Is Christmas Still

Phillips Brooks

The silent skies are full of speech
For who hath ears to hear;
The winds are whispering
    each to each,
The moon is calling to the beech,
And stars their sacred
    wisdom teach
Of faith and love and fear.

But once the sky its silence broke
And song o'erflowed the earth,
The midnight air with glory shook,
And angels mortal language spoke,
When God our human nature took
In Christ, the Savior's birth.

And Christmas once is
    Christmas still;
The gates through which
    He came,
And forests' wild and
    murmuring rill,
And fruitful field and breezy hill,
And all that else the
    wide world fill
Are vocal with His name.

Shall we not listen while they sing
This latest Christmas morn;
And music hear in everything,
And faithful lives in tribute bring
To the great song which
    greets the King,
Who comes when Christ is born?

The sky can still remember
The earliest Christmas morn,
When in the cold December
The Savior Christ was born;
And still in darkness clouded,
And still in noonday light,
It feels its far depths crowded
With angels fair and bright.

O never failing splendor!
O never silent song!
Still keep the green earth tender,
Still keep the gray earth strong;
Still keep the brave earth dreaming
Of deeds that shall be done,
While children's lives
    come streaming
Like sunbeams from the sun.

No star unfolds its glory,
No trumpet's wind is blown,
But tells the Christmas story
In music of its own.
No eager strife of mortals,
In busy fields or town,
But sees the open portals
Through which the
    Christ came down.

O angels sweet and splendid,
Throng in our hearts, and sing
The wonders which attended
The coming of the King;
Till we, too, boldly pressing
Where once the angel trod,
Climb Bethlehem's hill
    of blessing,
And find the Son of God.

Star-Kindled Lights
Florence A. Peterson

Christmas lights in varied colors
Decorate a fragrant tree,
Spark a light in children's faces,
Anticipating, endlessly.

Arch of lights, a dazzling splendor,
Rivaling Aladdin's dreams,
Give to streets a jewelled ceiling,
While below wet pavement gleams.

Lights embroider every dwelling,
Red and green and gold, they shine.
Candlelight on festive tables
Fantasies for Yule outline.

Long ago, above a manger
Shone a star whose wondrous might
Pierced the darkness, through the ages,
Kindling still, these Christmas lights.

The Jewel of Heaven
Marion E. McConnell

The Christmas tree, with tinselled charm,
wears costume jewelry on each arm;
but, atop its head, there spreads a pool
of golden light from a precious jewel—
a star, the diamond of the skies,
whose splendor ever signifies,
by its Holy light, to men on earth,
that our blessings stem from Jesus' birth.
These blessings, reflected, will always be
our most wondrous gift from the Christmas tree.

Photograph by Jessie Walker

Our Treasured Traditions

OF ANGELS, STARS, AND COWBOY BOOTS

Faith Andrews Bedford

Thirty years ago, when our first child was born, I gave him a special Christmas ornament. It was to be his very own. Over the years, I have filled the shoebox that holds his ornaments with special things that reminded me of him or marked an important milestone in his life. When his sisters arrived, they, too, were given an ornament each year. Slowly our tree became laden with wonderful, one-of-a-kind decorations rich with remembrance. Now, as we gather each year to trim the tree, we unwrap these treasured ornaments, laughing and reminiscing about the meaning behind each little keepsake.

The Christmas that our second child, Eleanor, was five, we had just had a new baby. That year, I found a wonderful angel holding the hand of a littler one. "This is you," I told Eleanor. "And the littler one is Sarah who is holding tight to your hand because you are going to be such a wonderful big sister." And she has been.

Because the ornaments belonged to the children, I have always allowed each child to unwrap their treasures and put them on the tree themselves, no matter how young they were. That they were sometimes used as toys shows. There is a feathered bird who is now rather bald, a wooden train with no smokestack, and a felt gingerbread man whose buttons have disappeared. Sometimes things that are well-loved look that way.

Eleanor always laughs as she unwraps her little angels, which have hung on the tree for twenty years, and remarks on the missing wing. "Was that an accident," she muses, "or a reflection on the fact that I have not always been angelic?"

She loves the crystal ballerina that I gave her the year she began ballet lessons. While the little dancer spins on her satin ribbon, Eleanor recalls the difficult choice she once had to make between becoming a professional ballerina or going to college. She chose the latter and has never regretted it. . . .

Our youngest, Sarah, was very attached to her teddy bear. Needless to say, bears abound in her ornament box—carved, china, stuffed. A sparkling golden bicycle marks the achievement of learning how to ride a two-wheeler and a replica of an antique plane commemorates her first airplane ride. For her fifth birthday she was given a kitten, whom she named Kate. That Christmas I found a little ornament with a fuzzy kitten curled up in a tiny straw basket.

Each year as Sarah carefully unwraps her ornaments, she fondly remembers our many trips together: the week in San Francisco where I found her the little wooden cable car, the visit to Hawaii marked by the straw palm tree. . . . Last year she remarked, "I'm not unwrapping ornaments, I'm unwrapping memories."

Drew, our firstborn and an enthusiastic athlete, has a stuffed felt soccer player and a wooden skier, a china tennis racquet and a carved kayak. As a child, his charging about the house earned him the nickname, "Drew the Dragon." So, of course, in his box is a intricately embroidered Chinese dragon as well as a green ceramic one from Mexico. . . .

Several years ago Drew married and moved out West. That year, of course, I gave him a little bride and groom to hang on his tree. As our first Christmas without him approached I climbed the winding staircase to the attic to look for the box of decorations. . . .

Behind a crate marked Wreaths and next to the box containing the creche, I found the carton marked Children's Ornaments. I opened it.

Drew's box was easy to spot; he'd drawn a big dragon on the top when he was eight. Taking off the lid, I unwrapped a few ornaments: the skiing polar bear he had gotten for his tenth Christmas and the Indian I gave him the year he became a Boy Scout. Then, I came across my favorite, a little pair of miniature cowboy boots I had given him the year his father had brought him back a real pair from Montana. Drew had refused to wear any other shoes for eight months.

I re-wrapped the little boots in tissue paper. Then, I carefully put everything back in the box and took it downstairs. In the warm kitchen, now fragrant with the armloads of evergreen boughs I had cut that morning, I wrapped up Drew's ornaments in brown paper and twine.

Long ago, when I gave my first baby his first ornament, I had decided that, when my children married and had homes of their own, I would give

them their ornaments. It was time to send Drew his. The little box was the seed from which his own tree of ornaments would grow.

I walked into the village to post the package, imagining Drew's surprise upon receiving it. As snow fell on the path before me, I smiled at the thought of the pleasure he would have telling his new wife about each ornament, its history and its meaning.

Last Christmas, Drew's gift to us was the news that we would become grandparents in a few months' time. Now, there is a new little person on my Christmas list; another generation of tree-trimmers has begun.

It will have to be just right, this first ornament for a first grandchild. Someday, as her father lifts her up to place it on the tree, he will tell her, "This is your very first ornament, given to you the year you were born." Then he'll point to a little star twinkling on another branch and say, "And that one over there; that one was mine." Her eyes will grow wide with Christmas wonder. A tradition will continue.

Featured Poet

Same Star

Eileen Spinelli

Come
all folks bedraggled
or frazzled
or wise.
Come winsome
or wild
with tears
in your eyes.
Come washers of windows,
come readers of books,
come keepers of secrets,
come dreamers and cooks.
Come out from
your corners,
hold hands in the snow,
and wait for the light
that lit hearts
long ago.

CAROL SINGERS *by Richard Telford. Image from DDFA.com*

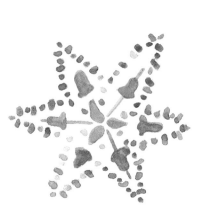

𝒞HRISTMAS IS A QUEST.
MAY EACH OF US
FOLLOW HIS STAR OF FAITH
AND FIND THE HEART'S OWN BETHLEHEM.
–Esther Baldwin York

Christmas
Faith Baldwin

The snow is full of silver light
Spilled from the heavens' tilted cup,
And, on this holy, tranquil night,
The eyes of men are lifted up
To see the promise written fair,
The hope of peace for all on earth,
And hear the singing bells declare
The marvel of the dear Christ's birth.
The way from year to year is long
And though the road be dark so far,
Bright is the manger, sweet the song,
The steeple rises to the Star.

The Eve of Christmas
Patience Strong

The Star that hangs above the hilltop glorious and bright
Might be the very Star that led the Wise Men
    through the night.
On the quiet air there comes a sweet familiar strain—
The sound of voices singing in the church along the lane . . .
Echoing the golden music of the heavenly throngs—
That heralded His wondrous coming with angelic songs . . .
To the stable by the inn the patient beasts are led.
The sheep stand in the frozen fields,
    the Star shines overhead . . .
This little English village in the starlight and the snow—
Might be Holy Bethlehem, two thousand years ago.

Word Made Flesh

John 1: 1–14

In the beginning was the Word, and the Word was with God, and the Word was God. The same was in the beginning with God. All things were made by him; and without him was not any thing made that was made. In him was life; and the life was the light of men. And the light shineth in darkness; and the darkness comprehended it not.

There was a man sent from God, whose name was John. The same came for a witness, to bear witness of the Light, that all men through him might believe. He was not that Light, but was sent to bear witness of that Light.

That was the true Light, which lighteth every man that cometh into the world. He was in the world, and the world was made by him, and the world knew him not. He came unto his own, and his own received him not. But as many as received him, to them gave he power to become the sons of God, even to them that believe on his name: Which were born, not of blood, nor of the will of the flesh, nor of the will of man, but of God. And the Word was made flesh, and dwelt among us, (and we beheld his glory, the glory as of the only begotten of the Father,) full of grace and truth.

FOLLOWING THE STAR *by Gordon Lees. Image from DDFA.com*

THE BIRTH OF CHRIST

Matthew 1:18–25

*N*ow the birth of Jesus Christ was on this wise: When as his mother Mary was espoused to Joseph, before they came together, she was found with child of the Holy Ghost. Then Joseph her husband, being a just man, and not willing to make her a public example, was minded to put her away privily.

But while he thought on these things, behold, the angel of the LORD appeared unto him in a dream, saying, Joseph, thou son of David, fear not to take unto thee Mary thy wife: for that which is conceived in her is of the Holy Ghost. And she shall bring forth a son, and thou shalt call his name JESUS: for he shall save his people from their sins.

Now all this was done, that it might be fulfilled which was spoken of the Lord by the prophet, saying, Behold, a virgin shall be with child, and shall bring forth a son, and they shall call his name Emmanuel, which being interpreted is, God with us.

Then Joseph being raised from sleep did as the angel of the Lord had bidden him, and took unto him his wife: And knew her not till she had brought forth her firstborn son: and he called his name JESUS.

NATIVITY SCENE *by Gordon Lees. Image from DDFA.com*

The Wise Men and the Star

Matthew 2:1–11

Now when Jesus was born in Bethlehem of Judaea in the days of Herod the king, behold, there came wise men from the east to Jerusalem, Saying, Where is he that is born King of the Jews? for we have seen his star in the east, and are come to worship him.

When Herod the king had heard these things, he was troubled, and all Jerusalem with him. And when he had gathered all the chief priests and scribes of the people together, he demanded of them where Christ should be born. And they said unto him, In Bethlehem of Judaea: for thus it is written by the prophet, And thou Bethlehem, in the land of Juda, art not the least among the princes of Juda: for out of thee shall come a Governor, that shall rule my people Israel.

Then Herod, when he had privily called the wise men, enquired of them diligently what time the star appeared. And he sent them to Bethlehem, and said, Go and search diligently for the young child; and when ye have found him, bring me word again, that I may come and worship him also.

When they had heard the king, they departed; and, lo, the star, which they saw in the east, went before them, till it came and stood over where the young child was. When they saw the star, they rejoiced with exceeding great joy.

And when they were come into the house, they saw the young child with Mary his mother, and fell down, and worshipped him: and when they had opened their treasures, they presented unto him gifts; gold, and frankincense and myrrh.

Bethlehem *by Gordon Lees. Image from DDFA.com*

The Little Christ

Nancy Byrd Turner

The stable roof was slant and mean,
The rushes on the floor spread thin;
There was no fire to warm Him by
When the little Christ came in.
There was no fire to warm Him by,
They laid Him in the prickly straw;
The humble, witless oxen saw
How helpless He did lie.

So helpless, and the stall so dim!
And yet, so near, the darkness riven
Of an archangel chanting Him
With cherubim and seraphim:
"Glory to God in Heaven!"

His tiny whimper brake above
The patient sound of Mary's sigh;
The drowsy cattle stirred to hear
The little Christ's low cry.
The silent cattle heard Him weep,
And waked, and lifted gentle heads;
Careless, nearby, on dreamful beds,
The inn-folk were asleep.

While, to their rocking camels bent,
Three dared the desert from afar,
One clear light in their firmament,
One cry among them as they went—
"The Star, the Star, the Star!"

Moonless Darkness Stands Between

Gerard Manley Hopkins

Moonless darkness stands between.
Past, O Past, no more be seen!
But the Bethlehem star may lead me
To the sight of Him Who freed me
From the self that I have been.
Make me pure, Lord:
    Thou art holy;
Make me meek, Lord:
    Thou wert lowly;
Now beginning, and alway:
Now begin, on Christmas Day.

Bethlehem of Judea

Author Unknown

A little child,
A shining star.
A stable rude,
The door ajar.

Yet in that place,
So crude, forlorn,
The Hope of all
The world was born.

Christ's Nativity

Henry Vaughan

Awake, glad heart! Get up, and sing!
It is the birthday of thy King.
　　Awake, awake!
　　The sun doth shake
Light from His locks, and all the way
Breathing perfumes, doth spice the day.

Awake, awake! Hark how the wood rings,
Winds whisper, and the busy springs
　　A consort make.
　　Awake, awake!
Man is their high priest and should rise
To offer up the sacrifice.

I would I were some bird or star,
Fluttering in woods or lifted far
　　Above this inn
　　And road of sin!
Then either star, or bird, should be
Shining, or singing, still to Thee.

Road in Deschutes National Forest, Oregon.
Photograph by Dennis Frates

While Candles Burn

Rowena Cheney

We meet tonight while candles burn
To praise our Savior King—to turn
Our thoughts to Him in quietude;
And in this Yuletide interlude
We say a fervent, grateful prayer
For all the blessings which we share.
This hallowed hour is sanctified
While candles burn at Christmastide.

How great our privilege—to light
Our candles on this holy night:
Each one ignited in the name
Of Him, the little Child Who came
To earth long centuries ago
To tell us of that brighter glow
Which candles are but symbols of . . .
Eternal Life and Peace and Love.
Oh, sing His praises far and wide
While candles burn at Christmastide.

Candlelight Service

Edna Jaques

How softly do the candles glow
In the dim darkness of the church,
Sending out tiny tongues of light,
As if upon a quiet search
For truth and beauty hidden there,
In the sweet atmosphere of prayer.

There is the smell of cedar boughs,
Of candle wax and drying fir,
The spicy breath of bergamont,
The scent of frankincense and myrrh,
As down the aisles the singers go
With their white candles all aglow.

The blessed music fills the church
With swelling tones of pure delight,
While the great organ flings aloft
The music of that holy night,
When shining hosts of heaven came
The birth of Jesus to proclaim.

The candles cast their flickering light
Upon the people gathered there,
The young and old . . . the rich and poor,
Their faces lifted up in prayer,
As faithful shepherds long ago,
They, too, keep watch by candle glow.

Detail from CANDLELIGHT *by Sam Timm.*
Artwork courtesy of the artist and Wild Wings

Bits & Pieces

The Christmas candle's waver-glow
In silence tints our window snow
With fragments of the brilliant light
Which haloed earth's first Christmas night.
—*George Knepper*

A silent psalm is candle flame,
Bright season's greetings to proclaim,
Lighting hearts that sing Christ's name.
—*Maxine McCray Miller*

O holy night, the stars are brightly shining;
It is the eve of our dear Savior's Birth.
—*Phillips Brooks*

A candle never is so small,
No night however dark
Can overcome a candle's light
When it shares the Christmas spark.
—*Eleanor Fiock*

A Christmas candle is a lovely thing—
It makes no noise at all,
But softly gives itself away;
While quite unselfish, it grows small.
—*Eva K. Logue*

As we proclaim the Christ Child's birth,
Our love shines forth in light
To form a halo around the earth
And bless this holy night.
—*Sarah Geneva Page*

Through stained glass windows candles glow,
Emitting warmth and light
To all who seek to worship here
Upon this holy night.
—*Loise Pinkerton Fritz*

Christmas Eve

Edgar Daniel Kramer

Christmas Eve! And lo! My eyes
See a star fill all the skies,
As its mystery of light
Leads the Wise Men through the night,
With the riches that they bring
To bestow upon their King;
While the shepherds hasten down
From the hills into the town.

Christmas Eve! And lo! I hear
Angels singing sweetly clear
Over meadow, hill, and glen,
"Peace on earth! Good will to men!
Turn from grief, all ye that mourn!
Christ in Bethlehem is born!"
And where sad-eyed cattle stir,
Mary's baby clings to her.

Christmas Eve! And lo! I kneel
Where the startled shadows reel,
With the Wise Men from the east
And the shepherds at a feast
In a lowly manger spread,
And partake of mystic bread;
While adoring makes us one
With God, Mary, and their Son.

Winter Night by Moonlight *by Randy Van Beek.*
Image from Applejack Art Partners

Christmas in the Heart

Margaret Williams Stevens

It isn't the tree with its tinsel,
Nor the lights blinking bright
  on the street.
It's the glow that we feel
And a joy that is real
As we wish well to all that we meet.

It isn't the gift or the giver
That makes this a season of cheer,
But the way we care
And the love we share,
That puts Christ in Christmas
  each year.

THE CHRISTMAS FEELING

The Saturday Evening Post

Christmas is a certain feeling. It is timeless, never quite absent any day of the year. But it quickens as the holly wreaths are hung and the gifts are prepared in the symbolism of love. At length it rises to the climax of the silent night, the holy night. Then men gather in sacred places, where their mood is tender with candlelight and prayers and gentle hymns about the One Who came upon a midnight clear. And in this openhearted moment He comes again, and men are flooded with a feeling He has always had about them. The feeling that no matter how imperfect men may be, deep inside their weaknesses and their errors is a yearning for perfection, an unquenchable brotherhood of goodness. What a hopeful, joyful, merry feeling it is!

Photograph by Miki Duisterhof/Botanica/Jupiter Images

A JOYFUL NOISE

Pamela Kennedy

The beloved Christmas classic, "Joy to the World," was penned by a man who, though only five feet tall, gained immense stature as the "Father of English Hymnody." Isaac Watts lived three centuries ago in England, penned over six hundred hymns during his lifetime, and revolutionized the singing of hymns in Christian congregations—he truly brought joy to the world!

As a boy, Isaac was precocious and something of a linguistic prodigy. When he was only five years old he began the study of Latin; he added Greek at nine, moved on to French when he was eleven, and attacked Hebrew in his early teens! He was writing poetry from the age of six. . . . By the time he was in his late teens, Isaac became increasingly bored and even irritated by the poor quality of Psalm singing in the weekly worship services he attended. Tired of Isaac's repeated complaints, his father finally threw out the following challenge: "Well then, young man, why don't you give us something better to sing?" The next Sunday Isaac did! And for the following two years Isaac Watts penned a new hymn every week. . . . In 1707, at age thirty-three, he published a collection of 210 original compositions titled, *Hymns and Spiritual Songs*. . . .

"Joy to the World" may not seem like a radical piece of work by today's standards, but in 1719, when it was published in Watts' second hymnal, it was quite a departure from tradition. In the eighteenth century, many theologians believed that tinkering with the words of Scripture came perilously close to committing sacrilege. In "Joy to the World," Watts not only paraphrased Psalm 98, but he also changed the original intent of King David's verses from that of an Old Testament song hailing the day when Jehovah, the God of the Israelites, would return and vindicate his chosen people, to a New Testament interpretation of Christ coming to earth as the Savior of mankind. Watts used the following verses from the latter part of Psalm 98 as the basis for much of his familiar Christmas carol:

Make a joyful noise unto the LORD, all the earth: make a loud noise, and rejoice, and sing praise. . . . Let the floods clap their hands: let the hills be joyful together before the LORD; for he cometh to judge the earth; with righteousness shall he judge the world, and the people with equity.

Although the words might be familiar to us, we probably would not recognize this hymn if we heard it sung in its original form. That's because the melody to which we sing Watts' verses wasn't composed until eighty-eight years after his death. In 1836, American teacher and choir director, Lowell Mason borrowed melodic elements from the German composer Handel's "Messiah" to set the English poet's words to music. It was an unlikely collaboration spanning two centuries and three countries, but today the message and stirring melody of this beloved Christmas hymn continue to ring true as millions of voices from all nations still "repeat the sounding joy!"

JOY TO THE WORLD

Words by Isaac Watts, melody by Lowell Mason

Joy to the world! the Lord is come; Let earth re-

ceive her King; Let ev'-ry heart pre-pare him

room, And heav'n and na-ture sing; And heav'n and na-ture

sing, And heav'n and heav'n and na-ture sing.

Because It Is Christmas

Eileen Spinelli

Expect surprises:

Darkness pulled
like taffy
into laughing light;

grace spilling
star-shaped
from your oven;

peace showing up
like a baby
on your doorstep;

songs knitted
playfully
into your socks;

angels rummaging
in your heart
for wings.

WET YOUR WHISTLE AND WARM YOUR TOES
*by Jane Wooster Scott. Image © Jane
Wooster Scott/SuperStock*

This Is Christmas

Patricia Emme

Golden candles burning bright,
Church bells ringing in the night,
Stockings hung with tender care,
Friends and family joined in prayer,

Tinsel shining from the tree,
Children singing merrily,
Holy star so bright above,
This is Christmas—God is Love.

ISBN-13: 978-0-8249-1320-5
Published by Ideals Publications, a Guideposts Company
Nashville, Tennessee
www.idealsbooks.com

Publisher, Peggy Schaefer
Editor, Melinda Rathjen
Copy Editor, Lauren Lanza
Designer, Marisa Jackson
Permissions Editor, Patsy Jay

Cover: Photograph by Nancy Matthews
Inside front cover: Painting by G. Coville Cravath. Image from Ideals Publications
Inside back cover: Painting by G. Coville Cravath. Image from Ideals Publications
Additional Art Credits: "Bits & Pieces" art by Kathy Rusynyk; "Family Recipes" art by Stacy Pickett
"Joy to the World" arranged and set by Dick Torrans

ACKNOWLEDGMENTS:

BALDWIN, FAITH. "Christmas." Used by permission of Harold Ober Associates, Inc. BEDFORD, FAITH ANDREWS. "Of Angels, Stars, and Cowboy Boots" from *Country Living*, Dec. 1996. Used by permission of the author. CROLIUS, KENDALL. "Sand Tarts" from *Around the Table*, by Lela Nargi, published by Penguin Group (USA), 2005. CROWELL, GRACE NOLL. "The Buying of Gifts." Used by permission of Claire Cumberworth. KIMMEL, HAVEN. "A Small-Town Christmas" from *A Girl Named Zippy: Growing Up Small In Mooreland, Indiana*. Copyright © 2001 by Haven Kimmel. Broadwood Books, Doubleday division of Random House. LEIMBACH, PATRICIA PENTON. "The Tea Set" from *All My Meadows*. Copyright © 1977 by Patricia Penton Leimbach. Published by Prentice-Hall. Used by permission of the author. PASTERNAK, BORIS. "The Christmas Pine Tree" translated by Eugene Kayden, The University of Colorado. RORKE, MARGARET L. "Christmastime Is Here" from *An Old Cracked Cup*. Copyright © 1980. Northwood Institute Press. Used by permission of Margaret Ann Rorke. THE SATURDAY EVENING POST. "The Christmas Feeling." Copyright © 1953 by the Curtis Publishing Company. SHARP-ANDERSON, SUSAN G. "In Search of a Christmas Tree" from *The Rocking Chair Reader: Family*

Gatherings. Copyright © 2005 by F+W Media, Inc. Used by permission of Adams Media, an F+W Media Incorporated company. STRONG, PATIENCE. "The Eve of Christmas" from *Happy Days*. Published 1952 by Frederick Muller, Ltd. Used by permission of Rupert Crew Limited, London.

Our thanks to the following authors or their heirs: June Masters Bacher, Deborah A. Bennett, Helen Darby Berning, Ruth M. Bryan, Rowena Cheney, Lucille McBroom Crumley, Patricia Ann Emme, Eleanor Fiock, Loise Pinkerton Fritz, Edna Jaques, Pamela Kennedy, George Knepper, Edgar Daniel Kramer, Marion E. McConnell, Maxine McCray Miller, Dorothy Minner, Sarah Geneva Page, Florence A. Peterson, Alice Kennelly Roberts, Irma Sanborn, Betty Wallace Scott, Laurence Smith, Eileen Spinelli, Margaret Williams Stevens, Nancy Byrd Turner, Daisy Wakefield, Elisabeth Weaver Winstead, Esther York Burkholder.

Every effort has been made to establish ownership and use of each selection in this book. If contacted, the publisher will be pleased to rectify any inadvertent errors or omissions in subsequent editions.